I0707486

Vermont Haunted History

by
William M. Alexander
Published by Vermonter.com
www.vermonter.com

© 2016 William M. Alexander. All rights reserved.

No part of this book may be reproduced in any written, electronic, recording, or photocopying without written permission of the publisher or author. The exception would be in the case of brief quotations embodied in the critical articles or reviews and pages where permission is specifically granted by the publisher or author.

Although every precaution has been taken to verify the accuracy of the information contained herein, the author and publisher assume no responsibility for any errors or omissions. No liability is assumed for damages that may result from the use of information contained within.

**Visit the Companion Website
Get FREE Extras!**
Vermonter.com has story updates,
photo galleries and videos that
accompany the stories in this book

Questions?
info@alpinewebmedia.com

Contents

The Bowman Family Mausoleum

If you're driving along Route 103 in Cuttingsville, Vermont, you might very well be momentarily startled. The eerie site of a ghostly white figure standing outside the door of the Bowman Mausoleum with a wreath and key in one hand, and a top hat in the other, is unusual to say the least. It's hard to miss, as it is located at the front of the Laurel Glen Cemetery. However, it is merely a statue of John P. Bowman, who along with his family, is interred within the walls of the huge stone vault.

In 1849, Bowman married Jennie E. Gates of Warren, NY, a dignified and well-mannered woman who was a devoted wife and mother and kind neighbor. The couple moved to Stony Creek, NY to establish Bowman's tannery business. A few years later, in 1854, a daughter was born and named Addie. Sadly, she died after just four months. A second daughter, Ella, became part of the family in 1860. She was to become a fine and respected young woman among the community.

Unfortunately, tragedy struck the family in 1879, when Ella became ill and passed away. Less than a year later, Mrs. Bowman also died, leaving her husband the lone survivor of his beloved family. In July 1980, the heartbroken John Bowman decided to construct a grand memorial for his family in his native Vermont. He found a piece of land near a burial ground in Cuttingsville, VT and hired a New York architect and designer to oversee his plans to construct a magnificent shrine to his deceased family. Over the course of a full year, more than 100 skilled sculptors, stone cutters, masons and laborers worked to build his Grecian style mausoleum. The cost at the time was $75,000 which was a fortune in those early years.

The final touch to completing the mausoleum was to add a life size statue of John P. Bowman himself, standing outside, holding a key to the family tomb. The eternal look of grief upon his marble face along with a mourning cloak, gloves and a funeral wreath, as he walks up the steps of the tomb are both sad and haunting.

In the year 1881, Bowman arranged to have three caskets containing the remains of his family placed within the tomb. He also arranged to have a greenhouse built upon the grounds, which would provide plants to decorate the cemetery. In fact, it was such a remarkable site that people would come to visit from miles away to picnic on the grounds. Inside the crypt is a life-size statue of his oldest daughter who passed away when she was only an infant. There are also busts of his wife and other daughter, who tragically died within just a few months of each other.

About a year later, Bowman hired a designer to construct a Victorian style mansion which he called "Laurel Hall", to serve as a summer residence, in the grandest of style. A spectacular fountain graced the lawn and a carriage house was built nearby. For ten years, Bowman entertained family and friends at his opulent home until he passed away in 1891 at age 75. He was buried within the mausoleum across the road, finally joining his family.

Bowman believed in reincarnation and left behind an unusual request in his will. A sum of $50,000 would finance the ongoing maintenance of both the mansion and the mausoleum. It was required that the house be kept in "waiting readiness" for him and his family to return. The custodian of the property diligently carried out his instructions keeping the clocks wound, a fire in the fireplace, and lights in the windows at night, along with a hot meal at dusk. The fund was depleted in 1953, at which time much of the furniture inside the mansion was sold at auction.

The Bowman mansion seems to be the focal point for hauntings. Those who rented the mansion after 1953 claimed that it was haunted. It was left empty for a period of time, which generated rumors that the home was haunted. Tales of weird noises and strange lights have been reported to manifest themselves within the mansion.

One tale told is the sounds of a phantom baby crying. The odd footnote to this is no children had ever lived inside the house, making this odd occurrence a mystery. As one might expect, strange and eerie experiences have been reported around the Bowman mausoleum at night as well.

Whether any of the above is true or not, the Bowman property, family story and especially the mausoleum are certainly unique.

For a period of time, a couple ran an antiquarian "Haunted Book Shop" at the mansion but it is now closed. As of this writing in 2016, the mansion is not inhabited and maintained by the Laurel Glen Cemetery Association.

Hope Cemetery – A Work of Art

Cemetery art and symbolism in the tranquil Green Mountains of Vermont? You bet! A trip to Hope Cemetery is quite a fascinating experience, though just a bit unusual. It certainly is unique! To view images of the monuments described below, visit Vermonter.com, where you will find a Hope Cemetery photo gallery.

Located on a small hillside in Barre, VT, the "Granite Capital of the World", the Hope Cemetery stands as a magnificent tribute to the stone cutters and artisans peacefully interred among their very own creations. Entering the front gate, you will pass by two granite sentries, forever watchful over their abode. From the moment you arrive you'll notice this is no typical resting place for loved ones gone by. It is truly a gallery of splendid artwork in the most unusual of settings.

Here's what distinguishes Hope Cemetery beyond the rest. Hobbies of the deceased are perpetually preserved through ornate stone carvings in the shape of soccer balls, bi-planes and even a racing car. Perhaps in consideration of the restful living, one monument is a life size easy chair with the inscription "Bettini".

One remarkably eerie tomb is shaped like a bed. William and Gwendolyn Halvosa are shown sitting up in pajamas, holding hands, their tombs stretched out before them. No doubt, preparing for what will be a very long night of sleep.

The "Bored Angel", also known as the "Sitting Angel", is the work of carver Louis Brusa. It rests between columns, legs crossed, head balanced on her chin. Brusa's own grave features a strange sculpture of "The Dying Man," slipping away, held by his wife. Brusa passed away in 1937 to a common stone carver's ailment, silicosis, from a lifetime of breathing in airborne stone particles. Ventilation equipment added to the stone carving buildings in the mid-1930s help to eliminate the hazard.

Another stone is carved in the shape of a bay window. A lady with a bonnet can be seen washing dishes next to a flower pot through the stone panes. Many other stones depict country scenes of Vermont highways, mountains and forests, beloved homes of the deceased and even a tractor trailer truck presumably the last reminder of a man named Galfetti. A tilted cube rests precariously on a stone base marked with "Tree of Life" and the inscription of "Salesman" on the adjacent side.

The truly awe inspiring statue monuments are perhaps the most ghostly of all. See Giuseppe Donati's stone, a raised relief depiction of a soldier smoking a cigarette, while the face of his wife or person close to him floats in a wisp of smoke.

Elia Corti has one of the Hope Cemetery's most fascinating stones of all. It was cut from a single piece of granite by the brother of the deceased. The outstanding hand carved life size figure sits quietly contemplative for an eternity to come. The detail of the clothing and the tools of the granite trade almost bring this figure to life.

Hope Cemetery was established in 1895. Originally, it contained 53 acres. Since then, it has expanded to a total of 65 acres. Edward P. Adams, a nationally known landscape architect, created the original plan for the cemetery. There are over 10,000 monuments made of Barre Gray granite. Hope Cemetery is a popular tourist destination and part of the Rock of Ages granite quarry tour.

Although it might be one of the more unusual attractions on the Vermont "must-see" list, Hope Cemetery in Barre, Vermont is certainly worth a visit.

The Middlebury Mummy

The last place you would ever expect to find an 8000 year old mummy is within the rolling hills of Vermont. Middlebury, VT's West Cemetery is the final resting place of an Egyptian Mummy. This story's origin starts in 1883 B.C., long before Vermont even existed

That ancient date, 1883 B.C., was when the young son of an Egyptian king, named Amun-Her-Khepesh-Ef passed away and was mummified for all of eternity. The mummy was the infant son of Sen Woset III, King of Egypt, and his wife Hathornhotpe.

So how did an Egyptian mummy end up interred in a small town in Vermont? During the nineteenth century when opening ancient tombs was popular, a US missionary was in Egypt and brought home the mummified body, as a souvenir. Rumor is that a local junk dealer, named Henry Sheldon, purchased the mummy from a New York antique dealer in 1866. He kept the mummy in his own house, along with a large collection of junk and trinkets (which eventually became a museum of sorts) until he died in 1907.

The mummy was exposed to heat and cold, dry conditions and dampness. Its wrappings were decaying and the embalming process caused the body to begin decomposing. The thought of a person left to rot in a Vermont attic was appalling to George W. Mead, a Sheldon Museum trustee. Mead wanted to give the boy, believed to be linked to Egyptian royalty, a proper burial. So Mead had little Amun-Her Khepesh-Ef cremated and buried with his very own tombstone, within the Mead family plot.

The Egyptian prince's grave stone is engraved with his name, the names of his royal parents and the date, 1883 B.C. In addition to the inscription, the stone bears three symbols, two of which are Egyptian for life and immortality. A Christian cross is inscribed between the two Egyptian symbols, perhaps reflecting the Christian burial services provided by the kindness of George Mead.

Pickled Post Mortem

University of Vermont medical students who graduated in the 1870's recalled the school obtaining cadavers from nearby cemeteries. This grisly practice was not all that uncommon during those early years in US history.

In other states that were less strict about how corpses could be treated, businesses sprang up that sold cadavers. This was particularly true of southern states, which shipped the bodies of blacks north to medical schools. The practice of shipping bodies had its drawbacks, though.

One UVM student remembered a body arriving from New York packed in brine in a barrel labeled "onions." The person, the students found out later, had died of smallpox. As a precaution, all the students were vaccinated the next day.

A Premature Burial in Vermont?

There literally is a "tomb with a view" at Evergreen Cemetery in New Haven, Vermont. Is it the case of one man's fear of a premature burial?

The fear of being buried alive is the frightening prospect of being placed in a grave while still alive. Most likely the result of being incorrectly pronounced dead. Before the advent of modern medicine the fear of premature burial was not entirely irrational. Throughout history there have been many cases of people being accidentally buried alive.

During the 17th century there were a number of premature burials. Collapse and apparent death were not uncommon during epidemics of plague, cholera, and smallpox. From contemporary medical sources, William Tebb compiled 219 instances of narrow escape from premature burial, 149 cases of actual premature burial, 10 cases in which bodies were accidentally dissected before death, and 2 cases in which embalming was started on the not-yet-dead.

Like something straight from an Edgar Allan Poe collection or a book of ghost stories, the plight of Dr. Timothy Clark Smith (1821-1893) is unusual to say the least.

Let's just say that although Dr. Smith has been dead for many years, things are definitely looking up...or at least he is. Dr. Smith was quite a busy man during life. He was a schoolteacher, a merchant, a clerk for the Treasury Dept. and obtained his degree as an MD in 1855, which led to his position as a staff surgeon in the Russian Army.

In 1893, Dr. Smith died at the Logan House in Middlebury, Vermont – on Halloween ironically enough. He left behind a wife and several children. Supposedly, he died with a fear of catching sleeping sickness, which would give the illusion of death, later to awaken in a cold, dark grave, very much alive. His body was interred at the Evergreen Cemetery in New Haven, VT, within a specially prepared grave.

Beneath the odd, grassy mound of earth, Dr. Timothy Clark Smith's face was positioned beneath a cement tube that led to the surface.

The 6 foot tube ended at a piece of 14×14 inch plate glass allowing Tim to gaze upward in the event that he was buried alive. An article by Joe Nickell of the *Committee for Skeptical Inquiry*, states that one of his children traveled to New Haven, VT from Iowa to supervise the construction of the specially designed crypt. According to the cemetery sexton, the burial vault has two rooms. One for Dr. Smith and the other for his wife. The burial vault is arched with stairs (capped by the stone in the lower front of the mound) and leads to the two rooms, with the viewing window at the top of the shaft.

Legends abound concerning the unusual tomb of Dr. Timothy Clark Smith. Did he really have tools buried with him to aid in an escape from the crypt, if he were to suddenly awaken? If you were to gaze down into the window these days, all you would see is darkness and condensation on the glass. People from years ago claim to have seen the skeletal face of Dr. Smith along with a hammer and chisel placed nearby.

Several reports claim that a bell was placed in his hand just in case he needed to signal that he was still alive. Which brings forth the questions...who could hear a bell under 6 feet of earth anyway? If he were alive, how long would the oxygen last if and when someone came to his rescue?

There have been many urban legends of people being accidentally buried alive. Legends included elements such as someone entering into the state of coma only to wake up years later and die again a horrible death. Another legend tells of coffins opened to find a corpse with a long beard or corpses with the hands raised and palms turned upward.

Fear of being buried alive was elaborated to the extent that those who could afford it would make all sorts of arrangements for the onstruction of a "safety coffin", to ensure premature burial would be voided (e.g. glass lids for observation, ropes to bells for signaling, and breathing pipes for survival until rescued).

An urban legend states that the sayings "Saved by the bell", and Dead ringer" are both derived from the notion of having a rope attached to a bell outside the coffin, which could alert people that the recently buried person is not truly deceased.

If you want to visit Dr. Timothy Clark Smith, take Rte. 7 to New Haven (a small town just a few miles north of Middlebury, Vermont). When you arrive in town, take Town Hill Road for about a mile or two. Look for Evergreen Cemetery on the left. The grave mound is clearly visible from the road and is about midway between the entrance and exits to the cemetery. Don't expect to see anything though. The glass view port is covered with condensation inside, obscuring anything (or anyone) visible below. Photos and videos are available at Vermonter.com.

Black Agnes

A copper statue located at Green Mount Cemetery in Montpelier, Vermont is that of a male figure, sitting with closed eyes looking upwards, his head covered with a shawl. Like many similar legends, "Black Agnes" supposedly is cursed with the power to some pretty vile things to those who may be tempted to sit on his lap. The list of not so wonderful circumstances include a certain death within seven days and a range of just plain, bad luck.

Dude looks like a lady! Black Agnes despite the name, is not really a woman! One thing remains a fact. The statue is bestowed with the title "Thanatos" (Greek for the word "death"). John Erastus Hubbard (1847 – 1899) was a Montpelier businessman with enough wealth to have the statue created and watching over his final resting place.

John Hubbard was a business man in the Montpelier area in the 1800's. It was said that he contested and inherited a sizeable amount of money from a wealthy aunt, (who had originally left the city of Montpelier a virtual fortune). He set about the task of building a public library for Montpelier, but at about 1/3 of the cost his deceased aunt had intended. Needless to say people in the area considered him greedy and mean spirited.

Did greed influence sinister activity in the afterlife? John passed away in 1899, at age 53, after obtaining his inheritance. The executors of John Hubbard's will were responsible for providing a monument to adorn his grave in Green Mount Cemetery. William Paul Dillingham, governor of Vermont from 1888 to 1890, took on most of the responsibility for finding someone to construct the odd monument, now known as "Black Agnes". It was created by Austrian sculptor Karl Bitter, who had run a studio in New Jersey.

The inscription on the wall framing the figure from the back, contains lines from William Cullen Bryan's poem "Thanatopsis" ("Thoughts on Death"), known to most all literate Americans of the 19th century:

Thou go not like the
Quarry slave at night
Scourged to his dungeon
But sustained and soothed
By an unfaltering trust.
Approach thy grave
Like one who wraps
The Drapery of his couch
About him and lies down
To pleasant dream.

No doubt that the "legend" is merely that, but the fact is that many people will not tempt fate and sit on the lap of the mysterious "Black Agnes".

Some of the reported odd occurrences surrounding "Black Agnes" included glowing red eyes at night, blood curdling screams and other creepy noises. Some people believe that the statue was haunted due to the misdeeds and demeanor of Hubbard, while he was still alive. Stories were told about a number of people who dared to sit in the lap of Black Agnes only to be found dead later.

The Search for Ethan Allen

In life, Ethan Allen was a controversial Revolutionary War hero that history often describes as fiercely independent, a bit crude, brash and undoubtedly, daring. Allen was no military genius, rather an overbearing, loud-mouthed braggart. He was also a staunch patriot who apparently did not know the meaning of fear. George Washington would write of Allen, "There is an original something about him that commands attention." On May 10, 1775, Ethan Allen with Benedict Arnold at his side led the Green Mountain Boys to capture Fort Ticonderoga on the New York side of Lake Champlain.

But where is this legendary figure now? It is known that he died on February 12, 1789, two years before Vermont was admitted into the Union. What most people believe is that his body rests under the eight-foot statue and the 35-foot granite column at Green Mount Cemetery in Burlington, VT. It's very easy to find. The monument is the tallest and most prominent one in the state. The whole structure stands upon a solid foundation of marvelous stone work. However, errors in the cemetery records indicate that Allen was actually buried 40 feet away from the site first identified as his grave.

Archaeologists excavated the area around Allen's grave, based on the cemetery plot map and found nothing at all. Many theories from grave robbers to a secret burial elsewhere are merely guesses. The truth is nobody really knows, for certain, where Ethan Allen is buried.

The Curse of Brunswick Springs

Ripley's Believe it or Not called it the "Eighth Wonder of the World" in 1984. To Abenaki American Indians, it is a sacred spot with natural healing powers.

Over the last two centuries, people with enterprising ideas have envisioned it as a place of business. Four hotel fires later, they were left to wonder: was it coincidence that led to their failure, or the curse of Brunswick Springs?

Brunswick Springs is located well off the main road in Brunswick, VT., a town of approximately 100 residents in the Northeast Kingdom. There are six individual springs at the spot, and each allegedly contains a different mineral-iron, calcium, magnesium, sulfur, bromide and arsenic-that flow into the Connecticut River 65 feet below.

The Abenaki Indian curse of the Brunswick Springs. The story of the curse begins in 1748, when Abenakis lived near the springs and relied on the natural healing powers of the waters.
When a soldier was wounded in the French and Indian War, his Abenaki companions brought him to Brunswick Springs. The springs were called the "Eighth Wonder of the World" due to the belief that the springs from the same source split into six unique mineral waters. "Legend has it that they brought him and put him under the springs, and lo and behold, he was cured," says Beverly Kettle, a resident of North Stratford, N.H., a town just across the river.
Kettle's father, Henry Savage, built the last hotel that fell victim to fire.

The soldier supposedly returned to the springs after the war to bottle and sell the water, and Abenakis objected to the sale of something natural. In the struggle that ensued, legend has it that an Abenaki man and baby were killed. The child's mother, a sorceress, is said to have cursed the springs. "Indians said anyone who tried to profit from the springs would fail," says Brendan Whittaker, Brunswick resident and chairman of the town's select board. He says the subsequent fires were caused either by "that curse, someone with a grudge or accidents."

Hotels rise over the water. As stories of healing continued to spread, the area began to look like a gold mine at a time when mineral waters were used frequently by the upper classes in Europe.

Kettle says the first house was built on the hill above the springs in 1832. The first hotel, called the Brunswick Spring House, followed in 1860. An early hotel brochure boasts the "medicine waters of the Great Spirit" and "60 guest chambers piped with the water from Brunswick Springs." The hotel stayed in business for several years. From the hotel, on the crest of a hill, the view included the Connecticut River, the Green Mountains of Vermont, New Hampshire's White Mountains, and Silver Lake, on which some say they have seen the ghost of the Sorceress. Others say the lake is bottomless.

"In the 19th century, people would apparently take the train to North Stratford (N.H.), and then a horse and buggy in to the springs, to the 'healing waters' as they called them," Whittaker says.

Dr. Rowell, a dentist, owned the hotel, and after he enlarged it in 1894, it burned to the ground.

He rebuilt shortly after the turn of the century and died in 1910. The land was sold to John Hutchins, who took over the hotel, then named Pine Crest Lodge. Three fires in three years soon aroused suspicion. Pine Crest Lodge burned in 1929, and Hutchins had two more hotels built on the land, in 1930 and 1931, before he gave up. Records list combustion of paint fumes in a storage room as the cause of one of the fires, but causes of the other two have never been determined.

"He thought it was a wonderful place," says Kettle, remembering what her father thought of the last hotel that he built. "North Stratford used to have a lot of hotels because of the railroad, but that was one of the nicest."

Nothing much remains of the Brunswick Springs hotel. A walk a quarter of a mile into the woods from Route 102 reveals Silver Lake first, now home to multiple beaver dams. Deer tracks cover the area after a recent snow. The ridge rises to the left, and a cement staircase, over a century old, can be climbed to the top, displaying a view across the Connecticut River.

Further in, another old staircase leads down to the springs, and visible on the embankment is an old, overturned springhouse. According to Whittaker, the small cement building is engraved with the names of several members of the Civilian Conservation Corps (CCC). The land around the springs served as a CCC site after the last fire in 1931.

Just past a clearing above the springs lay the remains of the 1931 hotel, a cement foundation and stairs leading down to a cellar. The place is still frequented and honored by Abenaki Indians, and they leave tokens of their appreciation and awe at the spot that is sacred to them.

Many people that live near the springs still believe there is a strange feeling to the place. Two men hanged themselves in the area, and one woman drove her car into the lake and drowned. Kettle says her brother found a man's body in a tree when he was hunting for partridge in the area and, as a small child, she sneaked down to see it. It made me sick," she says." He had hanged himself overlooking the lake."

Never to be developed again. If any enterprising businessman today ignored the curse and still wanted to develop the land, he could not. The Abenaki people now own the land and curse or not, it will never see development. "The Abenakis in Swanton formed a non-profit organization 10 or 12 years ago called Wobanaki, Inc.," Whittaker says. "They bought the land because it allegedly is a sacred spot for them." Wobanaki, Inc. then sold the rights to develop the land, through an easement, to the Vermont Land Trust on Oct. 22.

"A conservation easement is the right to develop land," says Kathleen O'Dell of the Vermont Land Trust. "It says that you can't add more buildings to the land or have other business operations besides those that already exist. As a land trust, we legally say that that land can't be developed again."

Healing powers: fact or fiction? There is no scientific proof of the healing power of the waters, or that there are even separate minerals in each spring. Whittaker says a state geologist from New Jersey tested the springs and found their mineral contents were not very different.

"If people want to believe the myth, and myth is not necessarily a bad word…, then fine. But scientifically, if you test the water, you'll find there's mostly sulfur dioxide, and its level is almost identical in each of the springs," he says. Legend and lore, however, do not rely or proof, and Bill Boudle, of Brunswick, says he needs none.

"I've been drinking that water since 1945," he says. "When I got out of the army, I went to work for the railroad and I hurt my back." Boudle says he went to doctors, chiropractors and tried anything he could think of, but believes it was the water that eventually healed him.

"I'm telling you that stuff will heal. A lot of people use it," he says…"My back used to hurt so I'd cry, but that's what did it: the Brunswick Springs." Kettle says that when she was a child, an old man lived in a cabin near the springs and walked in every day to get water. "He lived to be 90-something, or close to it," she remembers. "Maybe I need to go down there and start drinking that water."

Vermont's Deep Frozen Old Folks

Cryogenics in the snow covered hills of Vermont?

Vermonters are a frugal bunch and have been for many generations. In order to save energy during a long, cold Vermont winter, the truly ingenious old-time Vermont natives would find a way conserve food and heat....by freezing their old folks, for the duration of winter, and thawing them out in the spring time!

Maybe Vermonters were onto something long before science fiction made suspended animation worth consideration. These days, there are cryogenic laboratories freeze drying the heads and bodies of those who can afford it, but unfortunately (or fortunately!) due to cell damage during freezing, they haven't figured out a way to bring frozen folks back to life. Perhaps the old timers in Vermont can give them a few tips!

"A Strange Tale", describing this unbelievable ritual was published on the front page of the Montpelier Argus and Patriot, on December 21, 1887. The story, reported to be true, tells of a poor, northern Vermont family who had established the idea of putting their elderly and weakest family members into cold storage until they could be thawed out just in time for Spring planting.

The following is from a story by Wesley S. Griswold; from Mischief in the Mountains published by Vermont Life 1970: The Argus and Patriot listed the author as A.M. noting the events took place in a mountain town some 20 miles from Montpelier. A.M. wrote that the tale was excerpted from his Uncle Williams' diary.

January 7: I went on the mountain today, and witnessed what to me was a horrible sight. It seems that the dwellers there who are unable, either form age or other reasons, to contribute to the support of their families, are disposed of in the Winter months in a manner that will shock the one who reads this diary, unless that persons lives in that vicinity. I will describe what I saw. Six persons, four men and two women, one of the men a cripple about thirty-years-old, the other five past the age of usefulness, lay on the earthy floor of the cabin drugged into insensibility, while members of their families were gathered about them in apparent indifference. In a short time the unconscious bodies were inspected by several old people, who said, "They are ready." They were then stripped of all their clothing, except a single garment. Then the bodies were carried outside, and laid on logs exposed to the bitter cold mountain air, the operation having been delayed several days for suitable weather.

It was night when the bodies were carried out, and the full moon occasionally obscured by flying clouds, shone on their upturned ghastly faces, and a horrible fascination kept me by the bodies as long as I could endure the severe cold. Soon the noses, ears and fingers began to turn white, then the limbs and face assumed a tallow look. I could stand the cold no longer, and went inside, where I found the friends in cheerful conversation.

In about an hour I went out and looked at the bodies; they were fast freezing......I could not shut out the sight of those freezing bodies outside, neither could I bear to be in darkness, but I piled on the wood in the cavernous fireplace, and seated on a shingle block, passed the dreary night, terror-stricken by the horrible sights I had witnessed.

January 8: "We shall want our men to plant our corn next spring," said a youngish-looking woman, the wife of one of the frozen men, "and if you want to see them resuscitated you come here about the 10th of next May."

May 10: The men commenced work at once, some shoveling away the snow and others tearing away the brush. Soon the box was visible. The cover was taken off, the layers of straw removed, and the foodies, frozen and apparently lifeless, lifted out and laid on the snow. Large troughs made of hemlock logs were placed nearby, filled with tepid water, into which the bodies were separately placed, with the head slightly raised. Boiling water was then poured into the trough from kettles hung on poles nearby, until the water in the trough was a hot as I could hold my hand in. Hemlock boughs had been put in the boiling water in such quantities that they had given the water the color of wine. After lying in this bath about an hour, color began to return to the bodies, when all hands began rubbing and chafing them. This continued about another hour, when a slight twitching of the muscles of the face and limbs, followed by audible gasps, showed that life was not quenched, and that vitality was returning. Spirits were then given in small quantities, and allowed to trickle down their throats. Soon they could swallow, and more was given them, when their eyes opened, and they began to talk, and finally sat up in their bathtubs. They were then taken out and assisted to the house, where after a hearty dinner they seemed as well as ever, and in nowise injured, but rather refreshed, by their long sleep of four months.

Times change and the old traditions have a way of fading out. These days, we Vermonters just buy an extra pair of woolen socks and throw an extra blanket or two on top of Grandpa.

The Legend of "Johnny Seesaw's"

Johnny Seesaw's was built in 1920 by Russian logger, Ivan Sesow. Sesow called his enterprise "The Wonderview Log Pavilion" and began the legend with his wild Saturday night dances, homemade moonshine and rumored sin cabins out back. Throughout the roaring 20's, thanks to Prohibition, few lawmen and many loggers, "the Legend of Johnny Seesaw's" continued to grow. Around 1930, Sesow apparently bet the dance hall in one of his famous poker games, and lost. The buildings were sold and remained unused for some eight years.

In 1938 Bill and Mary Parrish bought the run-down property, constructed bunk rooms, installed plumbing, electricity, a kitchen and central furnace, and renamed one of the first ski lodges in the United States "Johnny Seesaw's." For the next four decades Johnny Seesaw's catered to thousands of skiers including a President of the United States, the first aviator to cross the Atlantic, Charles Lindbergh, and a bevy of famous and infamous personalities. At the beginning of World War II the concept of army ski troops originated at Johnny Seesaw's and eventually became the 10th Mountain Division. For forty years, Seesaw's, a renowned Ivy League hangout, offered lodging by referral only. If you didn't know someone who had stayed here, you didn't stay here.

Johnny Seesaw's operated for 34 years as a restaurant and lodging establishment but closed for business in 2014. In 2015, it went up for public auction.

The Hayden Family Curse

Legend has it that many years ago the entire Hayden family perished as victims of a curse.

In 1910, a horse drawn hearse carried the final remains of William Henry Hayden, last in the male line of his family, along the South Albany Road, to the village cemetery. Curtains were drawn across the mansion's windows in tribute, even though the extravagantly furnished house had remained without a tenant for nearly 20 years. Some would remember Mercie Dale's curse upon the family that the Hayden family name would die and pass into oblivion. What would happen now to the vacant, dark mansion with its wide fields and impressive barns? Was there a hidden family fortune and if so, where had it been secreted away?

Those answers and other secrets lie within the final resting place of Henry Hayden. Over the years, William acquired so much land that in 1823 he found himself in serious financial trouble. His mother-in-law, Mercie Dale had given him money over the years to help but it had never been repaid while he continued to ask for more. Suspicion set in and Mercie Dale became victim to a long illness, accusing William of poisoning her.

As the end came, Mercie uttered her ominous curse in the presence of her daughter, Silence: "The Hayden name shall die in the third generation and the last to bear the name shall die in poverty." In the final days, neighbor Sally Rogers cared for Mercie until she died. Her body was interred in the Rogers family cemetery as Mercie refused to lay within the same cemetery as the Haydens.

Once the new mansion was built, the Haydens enjoyed a privileged life that was the envy of the region. Pleasure rides in the horse drawn handsome carriages would often be the order of the day. There were servants to wait on family members. A New Year's Eve grand party would be held on the third floor ballroom.

For the most part, life was going well for the Hayden's and "the curse" was all but forgotten. Will and Azubah's daughters were all married and soon bearing grandchildren regularly. Though one son, William Henry (known as Henry) was more often than not erratic in nature and not very dependable. It wasn't long before things started to take a turn for the worse.

The curse continued to victimize the Hayden family. The only Hayden eventually left alive was Henry's daughter Armenia. All that was left of her inheritance was an unsavory family reputation and a number of unpaid debts. Due to illness and humiliation, she decided to live out her final days, in Waterville, Maine, where she died alone in poverty on February 20, 1927. She was the last of the Hayden family and the final victim of Mercie Dale's curse.

A Canadian family purchased the mansion and land for $25,000. Rumor is that the extensive bootlegging now took place within the estate, utilizing the underground tunnels previously used for smuggling Chinese. Public dances were held in the old ballroom as the new owners enjoyed their social status. Finally in 1922, the Canadians sold the property.

The fall of the House of Hayden. Over the years, each successive owner found the mansion difficult to maintain in the grand style it was accustomed to. During a period of hard financial times, the estate was sold off piece by piece, barns burned, the mansion fell into disrepair and the ell was engulfed by fire.

For many years, the mansion remained abandoned and was open inside and out to anyone passing by. Stories of ghostly activity and odd lights within the abandoned house were reported by people passing by over the years.

Some claim to have heard violin music resonating from the ballroom on a brightly lit, full moon evening in the summer. An interview with Dwight Dow, a descendant of the family, sets the record straight: "Ghosts? Hell no!!! Just some drunk passin' by in the middle of the night making up things. They had a ballroom floor, on springs, for dancing but they weren't no ghosts or none of that. Who's the damn fool that told you that anyway?" Dwight Dow passed away in 1976, soon after the interview.

The following is based on an interview with Helen Stacy of Albany, VT. On 6/10/2016:

Helen grew up at the Hayden house in the 1950's. She lived there for about 20 years, starting at age 11. Her family (Alfred and Goldie Mason) purchased the Hayden house for a mere $15,000 at the time. Helen said that there were a lot of fires at the property that seemingly started on their own. She recalls seeing a fire start in the roof of an outbuilding that started spontaneously while no one was in the area. She also recalls when the ell and carriage barn burned down, later replaced by the structure that's in place today.

Yes, the Hayden house IS haunted!

Despite the claim by Dwight Dow in a 1970's interview conducted with him, Helen claims that there were indeed paranormal activities taking place within the house. Although she doesn't believe that there was an actual curse, she did say that the Hayden family died out and that misfortune haunted the house for years after.

Two of the stories she recalls are as follow:

"My mother saw ghosts at least twice. The first time, she noticed a man sitting in the living room dressed in Lincoln period clothes with a hat similar to what Abraham Lincoln wore. She didn't believe what she was seeing and tried to ignore it. But, she had a little boy visiting at the time and the boy saw the man too. He called it "Pepere" (meaning grandfather in French) and approached it but the apparition stood up, walked toward the hall and then vanished."

"Another time, my mother heard old style ballroom music playing. It seemed to be coming from the dance hall in the upper portion of the house. Sort of like old fashioned waltz music. Curious as to where the music was coming from, she walked to the top of the stairs and the music just stopped and went away."

Asked if she knew of any other odd, ghostly happenings, she said "Well, I am 80 now, so I can't remember too many things but I do know that a lot of people would not stay at the house. Everybody in town knew there was something different about the Hayden house and most people didn't want to stay there."

The curse of the House of Hayden continues to interest and intrigue people from all around the world, even today.

The Lost Hiker Ghost

This story came if from our Vermont Ghosts & Myths Facebook Group and is quite intriguing. The article below was written by Jamie Ide and submitted by his wife, Emily.

If the date were closer to Halloween, I wouldn't bother posting this because no one would believe the strange encounter I had yesterday. I was hiking the Rock Garden Trail on Mt. Mansfield in the late afternoon when, after negotiating a tight passage, a sudden chill enveloped me. I reached down into my pack for a fleece and when I looked up I was startled to see a young man standing before me with a very concerned look on his face. His clothes looked well-worn and somewhat old fashioned, but I didn't think much of it at the time. I was about to say hello when he blurted out "Have you seen my brother? We got separated." I answered no and he replied "Well if you see someone on this trail, tell him I am looking for him" and was gone almost as suddenly as he appeared.

I didn't see anyone else on the trail and it was well past dark when I made my way through Nebraska Notch and back to the Stevensville Road trailhead. I stopped at the Underhill Country Store for a snack and asked the clerk if she knew of a lost hiker. Her eyes grew dark as she reached beneath the counter and withdrew a scrapbook which she opened before me. She flipped through a few pages and stopped on a small photo of two young men who appeared to be brothers. "One of these guys?" she asked. I can't swear to it, but the one on the left resembled the man I met so I nodded in agreement. Her finger slowly traced across the photo to a yellowed newspaper clipping that read "Search for Brothers Abandoned After Early Snowfall". The clipping was dated Tuesday, October 5, 1965. I raised my eyes to hers and she said in a soft voice "we never found any trace of my brothers."

Fifty years is a long time to be lost, long past the time that loved ones hold out any hope for your return. When I got home and looked at the photos from my hike, I found this one, which I don't recall taking. Perhaps fifty years is not long at all if you are well and truly lost.

Governor Grout's Ghost

by Sylvia Dodge (Courtesy of Scott Wheeler of Vermont's Northland Journal)

Travelers heading east on U.S. Route 2 out of St. Johnsbury drive through a small wedge of the tiny Vermont town named Kirby. On the left side of the highway stands a statuesque white house, and on the other side of Route 2 there is a huge old barn presiding over lowland cornfields alongside the Moose River.

Despite being in one of the least populated towns in Vermont (and Kirby also has only half of the acreage of most Vermont towns), the family that lived for generations along the Kirby stretch of the Moose River contributed a great deal to Vermont history. The Grout family lived in Kirby for at least four generations. From the Grout family came a Vermont governor, a United States Congressman, and a brigadier general.

History buffs in the area almost always refer to the big white house in Kirby as the "Governor Grout house"—and it is true that Vermont's 46th governor, Josiah Grout, spent a portion of his childhood in the home. It was his older brother, however, who made the Kirby property his home throughout much of his adult life. William Wallace Grout had a career of government service that most would say matches the achievements of his brother. He was a lieutenant colonel during the Civil War, was brigadier general of the Vermont militia, served in the Vermont Legislature, and also served in the United States Congress.

William Grout was laid to rest in the hillside cemetery alongside U.S. Route 2 that looks out over his Kirby property. From his gravesite you can see his stately home, the large barn he had constructed, and a riverside meadow thick with tall feed corn. The Governor Grout house is perhaps a misnomer. More appropriately, the stately Route 2 home should be called the Congressman Grout house.

Recent History and Ghostly Past

Much of the original Grout property in Kirby still remains intact, and has been owned since 1963 by Marc Poulin. On part of the farm—fields that once provided feed for the Grout family's cattle—golfers now enjoy the scenic, nine-hole Kirby Golf Course, which opened in 2001.

Mr. Poulin, now 86 years old, made his living logging large tracts of forest throughout the region, and in real estate deals. At one time he purchased a township near Jackman, Maine, and in a short time he turned a profit by selling the land to a paper company. On the Kirby property, he operated a company called Rus-Tique Brik, which he sold to a Quebec firm. The June 14, 1974, edition of the Montreal Gazette advertised the product as "now produced in Montreal." The antique looking bricks were made of a dense aggregate concrete. In its heyday 20,000 to 30,000 bricks were produced each day at the Kirby site and were dried in two large gas kilns located in the barn.

For over 200 years, the Grout–Poulin land in Kirby has been a property to be proud of, graced with the spirit of hard work, successful industry, and public service—and perhaps there are other spirits too. Although Mr. Poulin disavows that there is any sort of ghostly presence haunting his house, his children and grandchildren tell stories of spooky sounds and eerie shadows that have recurred through all of the generations that have lived in the home for the last half century.

It is believed that a woman who fell down a back stairway (the remnants of the stairway are now walled up) died in a bedroom in the old portion of the house. Four bedrooms are in that ell of the house, but they are used very seldom by family or visitors.

When Marc and Marietta Poulin moved their large family to the home, the youngest children were in third and fourth grade, and their bedrooms were located in the back portion of the house. On one occasion while going to bed, the two children opened the door to the ell, and heard a person moving in one of the rooms, but there was nobody there. Consequently, the two children slept into their high school years on a couch and a cot in the downstairs section of the house, refusing to sleep upstairs.

Recently, the caregiver who spends days with the elderly Mr. Poulin said that during times when her employer is napping in the afternoon, it is not unusual for her to hear footsteps over the kitchen, where the old bedrooms are located.

Perhaps all historic homes are haunted, but in the case of the Grout–Poulin property, the rich history of the site contains enough stories and spirit to fill the imagination. The next time you find yourself traveling east through Vermont on Route 2, take notice of the stately white house and barn in the tiny section of the highway that belongs to the town of Kirby, just east of St. Johnsbury. Think of it as the Congressman Grout House.

Ghosts at the University of Vermont

Burlington is Vermont's largest city and the University of Vermont is the state's largest university. Perhaps that helps to explain why it is also one of the most active hot spots of supernatural activity. It seems that the number of ghosts within the halls of UVM may sometimes rival the head count of the living student body, easily earning it the title of "Most Haunted College in Vermont".

The following are a sample of some of the spine tingling events that have taken place within the walls of the university.

The agriculture department (Bittersweet House) has a female ghost in period dress, circa late 19th century, who unexpectedly makes her appearance known. The Center for Cultural Pluralism (Allen House) reportedly has a ghost taking up residence on the top floor. Although he (or she) hasn't been seen visually, a cold presence can be felt in the vicinity.

The Center for Counseling and Testing is rumored to be haunted. The former director encountered the ghost of Captain Jacobs, a retired seaman who died there in the early part of the 20th century. Poltergeist activity, which is often described as "noisy ghost" activity has been reported there as recently as 1992. It would seem that Captain Jacobs is a restless spirit indeed!

The Grasse Mount House comes with a vibrant though eerie history of ghostly voices and doors that slam and lock themselves, without human effort. Converse Hall is reportedly haunted by a former student who committed suicide there. Though never seen, the student remains as active in death as he may have been while he was one of the living. He turns radios on and off and interacts with electrical equipment. The student electrocuted himself in 1998.

Coolidge Hall, a dormitory, has a few resident ghosts, including a male presence that likes to awaken the residents by staring at them, a playful spirit who enjoys pulling blankets off beds and a whistling specter that can't carry a tune.

The Millis Hall dormitory might have experienced a female ghost on the 2nd floor during the 97-98 year. Redstone Hall dormitory residents include a ghost that appears in the back staircase and has been seen to run through walls. He's not fond of female students for some reason (possibly pertaining to the circumstances of his death) and has chased frightened students out of the area on occasion.

At Simpson Hall, a spirit of a man who stalked a female student followed her to her dorm one year and apparently never left. He now resides in Simpson to this day. Late at night students wake up with a sensation of being watched. Usually the room becomes icy cold when it happens. Some students wake up freezing cold at night with the feeling that there is someone else in their bed.

The Haunted Railroad Bridge

If there is a haunted railroad bridge to be found in Vermont, the best place to find it would be in Hartford.

During a bitterly frigid winter night in the late 1800's, a fire occurred on the original railroad trestle in Hartford, VT. The Montreal Express, a train with passenger cars carrying 78 people, derailed and burned. Tragically, thirty-six people were crushed, drowned or burned alive, including a boy and his father. To date, this was Vermont's worst railroad disaster.

The old wooden bridge was eventually replaced with a steel structure on the original concrete footings. The bridge spans the White River and Route 14 in West Hartford. Tortured souls are said to re-live the gruesome event in perpetuity, a haunting and tragic tale to be sure.

It is said that people in nearby Hartford often avoid that particular section of road, near the failed trestle, late at night. Probably just as well, since the few who have rallied their courage to venture forth have come back in a near state of shock. The lingering scent of burning wood, a ghostly railway worker, and a small boy who materializes just above the river (as if standing on the ice), have been just some of the ghostly events encountered. Touching even the hardest souls are the plaintive cries for help, the wailing and screaming, as if those lost that night are reliving the tragedy over and over again, year after year. A truly haunting scenario doomed to repeat its ghostly, tragic origins for years to come.

Another Ghost Named Emily

Vermont has another ghost named Emily, though not as well-known as the famous "Emily's Bridge Ghost" in Stowe.

It is said that a ghost named Emily lingers on in the distinctive Marlboro College. A century ago, Emily Mather and her mysterious lover came to an end not unlike the story of Romeo and Juliet. Sometime in the late nineteenth century, back when the college was a working farm, Emily fell in love with a traveling salesman who called upon families within nearby Vermont villages.

Upon hearing the news, Emily climbed to the attic of her family's home and hanged herself. The home where Emily is said to have died is now known as Mather House, the college's main administration building. The stream where the heart broken salesman drowned still flows through the college campus.

Suicide at the time was considered shameful and embarrassing for family to endure. Emily was buried in an unmarked grave below her parent's barn, which was later remodeled into Dalrymple Hall, a building containing classrooms. Her body rested peacefully in the grave until the 1950's when excavation to build the Howland House disinterred her anonymous burial site.

It is the Howland House where unexplained occurrences have led some to believe that Emily's disturbed grave caused her spirit to walk among the living.

Students have reported seeing a female figure wandering the campus at night, and many have felt uneasy when alone in Howland or Dalrymple during the evening hours. Cold spots and banging noises (with no apparent cause) are often encountered around the campus.

Stowe, VT's Tap Dancing Ghost

Any self-respecting Vermont Inn has a resident ghost or two. The Green Mountain Inn located in Stowe is no exception. As a matter of fact, they have a very unique tap dancing ghost.

The Inn itself is more than 173 years old and during that time, it has welcomed a variety of guests from famous celebrities to the rowdiest of individuals. The Inn was also home to a local man named Boots Berry, whose life ended on the grounds of the historic Inn.

Boots was the son of the Inn's horseman and chambermaid. He was actually born at the Inn – Room 302 in 1840. During that time the room was located on the third floor as part of the servant's quarters. He grew up in and around the building and took over his father's work there in his twenties.

He became known as a respected horseman and caretaker of the Inn's horses. He was also responsible for providing fresh horses for the daily stagecoach. On one particular morning, the stagecoach team bolted and began to run away with passengers on board. Boots was quick to react and stopped the runaway stage, saving the lives of the passengers inside. He was awarded a medal for heroism and he became well known and popular throughout the county.

Unfortunately, his new found popularity also led to his downfall. He became unreliable and took to drinking and women, in perhaps an excessive amount of both. He eventually lost his job at the Inn. After that, he traveled the country and wound up in a New Orleans jail, where he learned to tap dance from a fellow prisoner.

At the beginning of 1902, Boots found his way back to Stowe. He was broke and only carried the tattered clothes on his back. Shortly after he arrived, there was a severe snowstorm which trapped a little girl on the roof of the Inn. Boots found his way to the roof and lowered the little girl to safety. Just as she was safe on the ground, Boots lost his footing on the ice covered roof and fell to his death. The roof he was on was directly above Room 302, where he was born. On

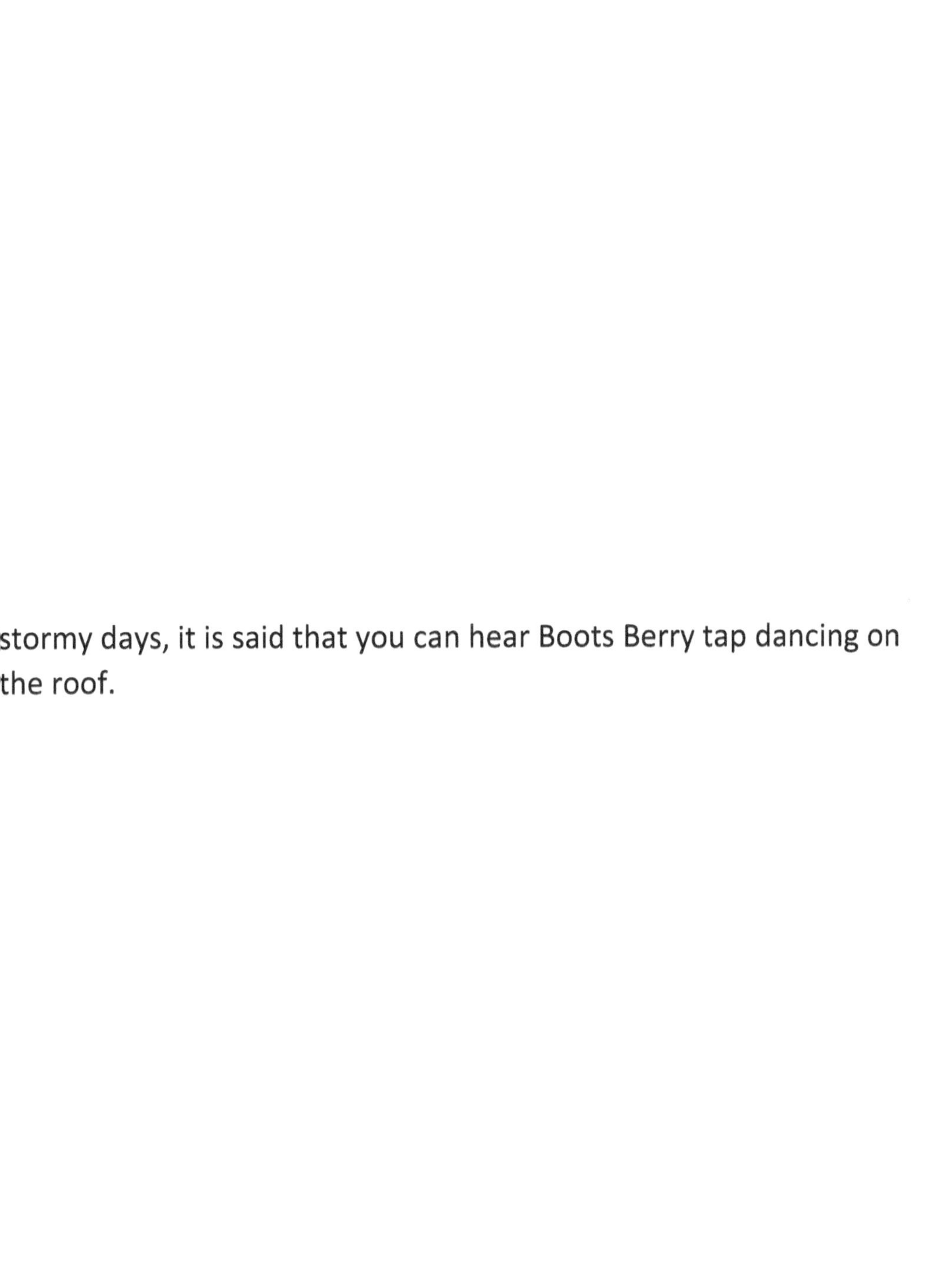

stormy days, it is said that you can hear Boots Berry tap dancing on the roof.

Spirits of the Highgate Manor Inn

The Highgate Manor was built in 1818 by Captain Steve Keyes along with The Manor Mayfair, which was located directly across the green from the Manor. During the period of the Civil War the Manor was used as a stop on the Underground Railroad with tunnels running from under the house to the river. These tunnels are still in existence today under the Manor.

The Keyes family owned the Manor until the year 1870 when the home was sold to Dr. Henry Baxter. As was the custom of the day, Dr. Baxter opened his practice in his home, the Highgate Manor. Bloodstains from his operating table are still visible on the wood floor in what is now the Library.

It was during this time that the legend of the Highgate Manor started to grow. Many of Dr. Baxter's children did not live past the age of ten and died of strange illnesses. The town's people believed that the good doctor was using his children for experiments and that after their death they have since remained in the house to this day.

After the death of Dr. Baxter in 1898 the Manor was taken over by Philip Schmitt and in 1917 the Manor was turned into an exclusive vacation resort. With business becoming an incredible success, Manor Mayfair was again added as part of the Highgate Manor along with the Manor Annex, and a brand new dance hall. This hall was billed as the largest and best dance hall in the North.

Due to the exclusiveness of the Manor, Al Capone as well as many other high profile dignitaries frequented the Manor Estate and its speakeasy hidden in a cave beneath The Manor. The Manor continued as a vacation destination during the 1940s. During this time Benny Goodman and other stars of the Big Band Era regularly performed in the Manor's ballroom specifically added for this purpose. Unfortunately, on May 22, 1950 part of The Manor's estate, the Manor Mayfair, was destroyed by fire set when a worker started burning leaves to close to the Manor.

Guests often report a strange presence in the basement bar (named after past visitor, Al Capone). Ghostly voices have been heard and some believe that the ghosts of Dr. Baxter's children still haunt the Inn.

In 2013, the author and owner of Alpine Web Media visited the Highgate Manor to take photos for a new website that was being built. "At the time, I was working with Jill Protzman and did a lot of the photography myself. The Capone Bar was fascinating and the tunnels mysterious. Walking through the rooms, you felt immediately transported to years gone by. The exterior was being renovated at the time and the Highgate Manor was looking spectacular. I was really excited about the new website design equally matching the new found ambience and look of the stately building itself."

"All was well for a year or so but ultimately, the owners Ben and Jill had problems paying for their web hosting bills. I worked with a lady who was their business manager and was a bit taken aback when she mentioned that the owners were having a tough time paying their bills."

"Finally, after a number of chances and notices the website was shut down. I hadn't realized the scope of legal issues that the owners had gotten themselves into."

"Several months later, I received a call from Ben Osmanson, the owner. He mentioned that a local TV station, WPTZ was doing a feature on the Highgate Manor and requested that the website be restored to take advantage of the exposure. He paid his past due bill and it appeared that the situation was improving. Unfortunately, that was not to be and the grand future of the Highgate Manor fell like a house of cards as Ben Osmanson's problems with the FBI were well under way."

The rest they say is history as the Highgate Manor slipped back into disrepair and was eventually sold at a real estate auction.

Although the ghost stories and hauntings are of interest, this latest saga is perhaps the most disheartening of all. It really was a gorgeous place. The Highgate Manor was empty for a number of years afterwards but eventually purchased as a private residence. The current owners are reluctant to discuss the manor as of this writing.

Most Haunted St. Michael's College

St. Michael's College is located in Colchester, VT. It's one of those colleges you drive by all the time and admire the beauty of the historic buildings. Seemingly, a picture perfect campus with a typical Vermont look and appeal. But are there strange things going on behind locked doors?

St Michael's (or St. Mikes, as it is known locally) campus may have ghostly inhabitants. The theater supposedly is haunted by a long dead nun who assists (or more likely frightens) actors. Incidents have been reported of props mysteriously disappearing, during performances, with no explanation. Some claim that the men's first year dormitory also houses an evil presence. In fact there are many paranormal stories about St Michael's College including curses, ghosts, a disembodied arm and even an ax massacre alert in the area.

A rumor persists that in the 60s or 70s, young men were taking part in some sort of occult rituals within the walls of St Mikes. During one such covert meeting, a participant claims that he needed to close the "portal" before everyone involved in the ritual left, but by that time security had arrived and the group was escorted off campus. The door to the attic is padlocked shut. However, eerie lights have been seen in the attic. Footsteps have been heard in the middle of the night by residents sleeping on the top floor. Joseph A. Citro confirmed in his book *Vermont Haunts*, the pentagram does indeed exist. As of 2011, the image of the pentagram still appears on the floor despite attempts to remove it.

Jonathan Wheelock's Haunted Farmhouse

Deacon Jonathan Wheelock's farmhouse was constructed in 1789, when he founded the first Episcopalian church there. Born at Shrewsbury, MA, 1727, Wheelock was a Minuteman in the Revolution. He married Anna Drury in 1753, and in 1789 moved to Cavendish, Vermont. He owned 1,038 acres of land in Cavendish Center and District No. 3. Deacon Wheelock divided his land among his children so that each would have a farm, visible from his own farmhouse. Obviously Jonathan was a man who liked to keep his family and home closely knit.

Jonathan Wheelock was allegedly the victim of a violent accident that took his life. He died on August 13, 1842. But perhaps Jonathan chose not to cross over and now still resides within his haunted farmhouse, watching over others. Poltergeist activity has been reported (objects moved to other locations and between rooms when no one else was present in the house, objects falling off shelves, etc.), which ultimately resulted in ghostly sightings. On some occasions, witnesses report waking up and seeing an opaque shadow form, or something human shaped looking gazing upon them or leering out nearby windows. Perhaps Deacon Jonathan Wheelock is still watching over his farmhouse, even in death.

Goddard College's Musical Ghost

A ghost with a talent for music is reputed to occupy the Manor House at Goddard College in Plainfield, VT. A prospective student walked into the Manor House, only to find a man playing the piano. The student asked the man for directions but the question was ignored, while the strange man continued to play. The perplexed student walked out in frustration. She was heading into the upper garden when she turned around and noticed the mysterious piano player laughing at her. The unusual specter then vanished into thin air.

Who could the mysterious piano player have been? Similar stories have been reported by others who visit Manor House. There are also recent reports of other unusual occurrences, such as camera malfunctions and orbs of light at Manor House as well.

Bennington's Most Haunted

Southern Vermont College (formerly known as the Edward Everett Estate) is located in the picturesque village of Bennington, VT . Everett's fortune was made from becoming the first person to strike oil in Ohio. He married Amy King, the daughter of a wealthy businessman. He built the Estate as a summer mansion in Vermont. According to legend, not long after the estate was built, Everett's wife Amy, drowned while swimming. Others would claim that her death was a suicide or even a murder. The "official" story as reported, was that she died at their other home in Washington, DC from a prolonged illness, dying during a serious operation.

Everett remarried in 1920 but his three daughters with his first wife, Amy, never got along well with Grace Burnap, his new but younger wife. This resulted in conflict and legal battles when Everett passed away in 1929. The affair over his will was so bitter that it became known as "The Battle of the Bennington Millions", as it was the largest court case in Vermont. Such a contentious and emotionally charged history perhaps laid the groundwork for the Estate's paranormal events to come.

The estate became the site of St. Josephs School, a Catholic seminary that closed and became a co-ed college (Southern Vermont College). Some report the ghostly presence of a woman dressed in white who roams the former estate and grounds. She is believed to be the spirit of Everett's first wife who had died so mysteriously. A couple by the name of Lundoff, lived near the Everett Estate in 1956 and ended their existence in a double suicide. This sad event could only serve to increase the negative energy of the area.

According to years of students/staff performing night security, ghostly activity could possibly include Everett himself, his second wife, Grace, and mysterious persons wearing black hooded robes (seen quite often around the area). Common paranormal activities reported, include: smoke filled hallways, lights turning on in rooms that are locked, doors/windows unlocked after being secured during a previous security round, footsteps around the college when no one else is in the building. The 2 main sources of paranormal events in the estate are the 3rd floor and an Abbey room with a strange energy. The second source (now a classroom), was the sleeping quarters for house staff where a maid supposedly hung herself.

Lake Bomoseen's Ghostly Rowboat

The town of West Castleton now sits abandoned, but it was once home to Irish immigrant slate workers who were fond of crossing Lake Bomoseen to visit a tavern on the east shore. One night, three men set out for a night of carousing. They never returned. The next morning, their boat was found floating empty. Their bodies were never found. Today, lakeside residents claim that sometimes during a full moon, a dark, unoccupied and ghostly rowboat can be seen moving silently across the lake toward the West Castleton Bay. No oars disturb the otherwise glassy, still surface.

Shelburne Museum's Resident Ghosts

Shelburne Museum located on Route 7 in Shelburne, VT. is probably one of Vermont's best known tourist destinations. Each building is filled to the brim with Americana and artifacts from the distant past. At least one of the old buildings on the museum's sprawling grounds, the Dutton House, may contain something a bit more paranormal than historical.

The Dutton House was built in Cavendish, Vermont, in 1782, and was unoccupied for forty years. It was donated and moved to the Shelburne Museum in 1950. From the outside, it looks like a charming, red New England colonial with a well-manicured walkway to the front door. Once you walk inside, the musty scent of the past and the creaky floorboards quickly capture your attention. Perhaps there is more to this house than meets the eye?

It is said that the Dutton House contains a resident who refuses to leave, although he has been dead for many years. One museum employee reports that on her first day on the job, as a tour guide, she went upstairs and noticed an older man with a white shirt and scruffy face hunkering down under the slope of the roof. Another museum tour guide mentioned that she has heard the sound of a little girl crying.

Reportedly, there are some employees who fear and refuse to enter the Dutton House. However, there are a number of people who make a beeline for the old house, hoping for a glimpse of its ghostly resident.

The Hildene and Equinox Lincoln Ghosts

Manchester, VT has some very historic buildings with perhaps a spirit or two lurking in the shadows. Mary Todd Lincoln and her children from Washington D.C., spent two summers at The Equinox, a luxurious hotel, built in 1769, in Manchester Village, VT. The assassination of Abraham Lincoln ended the families plan to return there for the summer of 1865. The Lincoln family's association with the Manchester area grew with son Robert Todd Lincoln's purchase of neighboring estate Hildene.

Guests have reported unusual activity and other worldly events at the resort. The typical recipes for a haunting including shadows that move quickly out of the corner of the eye, ghostly whispers and cold spots in various places within the hotel. Strange lights have been seen along with the general feeling of "not being alone". Due to the age of the resort and its long history, some of these events could be attributable to common non-paranormal activities.

Employees at the Hildene have allegedly seen ghostly shadows on the third floor, of a woman and a child that coincide with descriptions of Mary Todd Lincoln and one of her sons. What other ghostly phenomena lurks within the magnificent Hildene? The Equinox most likely has its own spirit activity as well. Perhaps through their visits the Lincolns are trying to recapture the care free days of those summers.

Ghosts of the Norwich Inn

The Norwich Inn was the first tavern in Vermont to entertain a President of the United States.

On July 22, 1817, President James Monroe stayed at the hotel.

Is the Norwich Inn haunted? The Norwich Inn is a one of a kind, historic Vermont hotel that dates back to 1797, when it was constructed. It was built upon land owned by Colonel Jasper Murdock, a graduate of Dartmouth College, who built his home at what is now the corner of Main Street and Beaver Meadow Road.

It has been said that numerous guests have walked the halls and stayed at the Norwich Inn, but some may have never checked out. The Inn was purchased by Charles and Mary "Ma" Walker in 1920. According to the local legend, Ma Walker kept up the Inn's tradition as a tavern throughout the prohibition, by selling bootleg liquor from the basement, even after husband Charles' death, until the mid-1930s, when her own health concerns forced her to sell and retire from her life as the innkeeper.

After Mary passed away, her spirit was apparently seen gliding along the upper floors. Her spirit can sometimes be seen in the dining room, dressed in a black formal gown. The lady wearing a long black skirt, is said to have been seen wandering through the building's parlor, eventually disappearing into the adjoining library. She also seems to have a particular fixation on room 20 where many unexplained events take place.

The apparition has also been seen in the guest rooms. Is it Ma Walker or perhaps yet another ghostly resident of the Inn?

Other ghostly phenomenon include toilets flushing themselves, faucets turning off and on, and rocking chairs eerily rocking away with nobody sitting in them. If it's Mary, she certainly is a bit mischievous type of ghost!

Innkeeper Andy Aldrich once reported that "the guests tell me basically the same story." Here are a few of his recollections:

A guest will say, "I heard some people who arrived very late last night in the room across the hall from me. I heard them speaking and talking about the really good time they just had." This is in a context of having been to a dance or party.

Guests have often asked, "Who were the people who came in late last night, talking loud enough so I could hear their words? And where did they go to a party?" Another guest version of a similar query, "I heard the people across the hall from me last night talking and laughing and speaking about how happy they were."In all of these instances, it's in reference to the same room, always late at night, and with similar descriptions as to what they heard the other guests saying. Oddly enough, there were no guests across the hall.

They, the real guests, were the only ones in a room on that stairwell. I myself have heard what I thought were people up in that room when I know I haven't registered anyone in that room. I go to look and don't find anyone. So it's a very nice couple who happen to be spirits. Yes?

Vampires in Woodstock, Vermont?

A vampire's heart burned on the Woodstock, VT village green? Maybe. There is a well-known legend that suggests that in 1834 the eldest son of the Corwin family of Woodstock, VT died from a mysterious wasting disease. When another son became ill, townspeople of Woodstock advised the Corwins to take precautions against a vampire.

According to legend, the eldest brother was disinterred from the Cushing Cemetery and burned. His ashes were buried in an iron container beneath the Woodstock village green. Supposedly, a few local boys decided to get together late one night and dig up the burned ashes.

They quickly abandoned their grisly task when they heard unearthly screams and voices all around them. This may all be typical New England folklore as the town register does not contain any records about a Corwin family, who were born or died, held land plots, etc. in the Woodstock community. Were there any vampires buried on the Woodstock green? If so, no one has yet found any evidence to confirm it. Maybe this is one well spun VT vampire legend without much bite!

Burlington's Restless Spirits

There are many locations in Burlington, VT with a ghostly history of hauntings and paranormal activity.

The story goes that a man who once worked at the former Carburs Restaurant building (now known as American Flatbread) killed himself in the basement. The bullet went through his head and into a nearby wall. Supposedly, you can still see the bullet hole in the basement. Most encounters happen in the basement, which houses the kitchen and tapped kegs under the bar.

Waitresses reported their skirts being lifted up from a cold wind. Doors have slammed closed, trapping employees in the basement's walk-in. Waitresses were told not to go down in the basement. The basement is also connected to other old buildings in downtown Burlington by various tunnels from the prohibition era. There are a lot of reports of phantom voices throughout the restaurant when no one is there. The ghost seems to specifically taunt women. Reports of breaking glasses, plates flying off of counters and sudden increased oven temperatures were not uncommon. A female bartender reported a pyramid of water glasses appearing on the bar, right after she had put the glasses away and turned her back for a second.

Old Stagecoach Inn's Ghostly Guest

The Old Stagecoach Inn is an historic bed and breakfast built in 1826, located in the center of Waterbury Village, VT. Formerly a tavern, stagecoach stop, and private residence, it is currently listed in the National Register of Historic Places.

Is there a "ghost in residence" eternally occupying the Inn? Room is reportedly haunted by a lady named Margaret Spencer who supposedly died there. Built in 1826, by a wealthy millionaire, It has served as a tavern, stagecoach stop, and a private residence and is now one of Waterbury Vermont's most well-known historic Inn. In 1890, the Old Stagecoach Inn underwent its first character structural transformation "from New England Federal to Victorian, an aspect that was meticulously restored in 1987 as an example of country elegance," which can be seen in great detail in its elegant parlor or in the cozy library bar.

The Old Stagecoach Inn has three floors. In the downstairs area, there is a large parlor with original antiques, and the rooms throughout the inn also have era antique sofas, easy chairs, organ, tapestries, and oriental carpets. The second and third floors, where the guest rooms are, there are 8 uniquely different rooms, and 3 more modern suites with TV, Cable, eat-in kitchen alcove and private bath.

During the 1920's, through the '40's, the Old Stagecoach Inn was the private home of a wealthy socialite, Margaret Spencer. In 1947, Margaret died at the age of 98, in her own bedroom, which is known as Room 2. Margaret Spencer loved her home so much, she chose not to move on to the other side, but instead decided to haunt old bedroom, appearing occasionally to startled guests, wearing a white shawl. Margaret Spencer apparently has no plans to ever leave and has made no effort to do so. However, she seems to be willing to share her room with the living, though the living may find a ghostly roommate slightly unnerving.

Some people pass on but are so attached to their past lives that they choose to remain here, and walk among the living. This actually fits in quite well with the Vermont folklore that often boasts that an old house is not really the genuine article unless there is a ghost in residence.

The Old Stagecoach Inn would seem to be the epitome of such folklore. There is a long history and stories of strange goings on there, which the new owners may have dismissed as products of the imagination. But as time passed a continuing series of "happenings" most likely forced them to reconsider.

These "happenings" are mostly minor, almost practical jokes, as though someone or something were having fun with a perplexed housekeeper or guest. They would occur as often as not, in broad daylight with living people present, at other times in the dead of night. For example, a rocking chair may begin to rock in an agitated manner, continuing for a while with no one near it; furniture items move on their own; beds have their linens stripped and neatly folded while the housekeeper is working nearby, plus other similar incidents too numerous to mention. The "ghosts" seem to be playful though and not malevolent. The only ill effects have been a reluctance of cleaning staff to work alone upstairs.

Ghosts of the Back Inn Time

Friendly resident ghosts are said to have made the St. Albans, VT., Back Inn Time (a local inn) their home. According to Pauline Cray, who owned Inn in 2012, there is Lora, the wife of Sidney Weaver, a past owner of the home, haunting the Inn. Lora died at the young age of 30, however her spirit reportedly lives on at Back Inn Time. Another ghost spotted is that of a man. He has been seen in the downstairs parlor.

Ghost hunters at the Back Inn Time.
Guests, including teams of paranormal investigators, have claimed to have heard voices, noises, or even seen apparitions while staying at the Inn. Unexplained noises and voices were heard and recorded during a session in 2009, by a group known as the Vermont Spirits Detective Agency.

Built in 1858 by Victor Attwood, the building has seen some rich history. This beautiful Victorian manor was built in 1858 by Victor Atwood in the old Railroad town of St. Albans, VT. The house is rare, in that it has only had 3 owners, prior to the Cray family.

Despite only one man being documented as dying in the building, patrons claim to see an older woman. The man who passed was a descendant of Victor Attwood, and the last owner in the family until purchased by the current owners. One unusual story is that psychics determined that the land was once used as a site for child slavery. There was also mention of a mentally challenged person being locked in a windowless room within the Inn.

In 2008, the Cray family hired Alpine Web Media to construct a new website for the Back Inn Time and take numerous photographs around the Inn. Like the nearby Highgate Manor Inn, also photographed for a website, no signs of unusual activity was experienced. Pauline Cray used to sponsor "Mystery Weekends", a Halloween "haunted house" and other events to promote the Inn during her ownership.

Pauline Cray sold the Back Inn Time Inn around the year 2012. The new owners of the Back Inn Time, claim that there is no supernatural activity of any kind taking place, since they purchased the Inn.

Ghosts Visit the Cahoon Farm

by Denise Brown courtesy of Scott Wheeler

My children swear I didn't tell them about the ghosts before we settled into what I've come to learn is one of Lyndon's most famous haunted houses.

Maybe that's true. Their father had died, and I was eager to move from Connecticut, and didn't feel that a few spirits lingering about should deter us. But in truth, I didn't put much stock into the stories the realtor told me anyway.

The old house had stood empty for several years. The shutters, those that remained, were broken and askew; the shrubs overgrown; one door was boarded up against the weather. Dark stains on the ceilings signaled the roof needed serious repair. The heat and electricity were off, and the air that hung in the dusty rooms was as bitter cold as that outside. But I fell in love with Cahoon Farm moments after I walked inside.

It felt like I'd come home. I hadn't really.
Cahoon Farm, built in 1798, had stayed in the Cahoon-Hoffman family for two centuries. You could say it still has, given its historical importance and our occasional nighttime visitors. Over our five years here, I have come to think that at best we're sharing the property. But I think that's true for anyone who purchases and attempts to preserve a historic home. We become caretakers of the past.

The previous owner, Horty Hoffman, was an historian herself, and in the early seventies had lovingly and authentically papered and appointed the old homestead, and conducted numerous house tours and field trips for students from the graded school. I don't try to keep pace with Mrs. Hoffman's efforts, but it has been a pleasure now and then to open our home to visitors, reporters, and students. And while many are intrigued by the ornate woodwork in the formal parlor, the wide pine planks in the hall, or the spacious symmetry of the rooms, the first thing almost everyone asks is, "Have you seen any ghosts?"

Quite a few people have over these two centuries. Ghosts still visit Cahoon Farm.

We should begin at the beginning, with the story of Daniel Cahoon, Sr., who in September of 1811, was gored to death while rescuing a child from a bull. Ol' Dan'l was laid out in an upstairs bedroom known as the Green Room, and it's his ghost who is said to be heard tromping up the stairs some evenings. And what he's looking for is also the stuff of folklore—a wine cellar supposedly boarded up by his grieving widow, who was convinced it was a potent drink that brought about her husband's demise. People have been searching for that cellar ever since. And so has Dan'l, according to legend.

In other stories, overnight visitors have been awakened by ghosts: one supposedly played a bit of tug of war with one guest's blankets, and another held his head in his hands and mourned the drowning of his young son. Clayton Homman, Dan'l's descendant who rarely talked about ghosts, is said to have seen one himself by his bedside—a young woman in old-fashioned dress. Some have heard music playing and glasses tinkling in the parlor that once held the first piano in Lyndon. A young couple dressed for a wedding—the woman in white, a man in top hat and black jacket—showed up one morning in that upstairs Green Room, which at one time could be expanded into an area fit for ceremonies and balls by lifting up a retractable wall.

I suppose skeptics and psychologists could have a field day explaining away such sightings as the products of over-stimulated imagination or worse. And I don't want to give the impression that these sorts of things happened regularly in this old house. In our five years, we've experienced relatively few mysterious happenings: an electric fan that turned itself on several times, for example, sudden volume changes of the television set, or doors that open and shut by themselves. Things that go bump in the night. All manner of occurrences that could be explained away as power surges, or the creaks and groans that accompany the settling of an old house.

But I have one story to tell. See what you think of this. Shortly after I moved into the house, I decided to have the kitchen counter top replaced. The morning this work was completed, I was standing at the sink, running a dishtowel over the new counter, happy with the job. And I saw a figure float by the kitchen door. She was a bit taller than I, all draped in what seemed to be black lace. And my immediate thought was, "There's the widow of the house checking on the new widow of the house." I stepped into the hallway, but she was gone.

A few weeks later, a good friend came to visit. Late in the evening, her daughter went downstairs to get a glass of water from the kitchen, and in roughly the same area of the hall, she saw a woman standing before her. The following morning, she sketched her for me, describing the very figure I had seen: a woman of the same height, the same lace covering head and hands.

I'd not said anything to my friend or her daughter about the woman in black.

A few years later, I decided to replace the worn linoleum in the kitchen. And the morning that job was completed the lady returned. Only this time I saw her floating by the doorway all in white radiant. Perhaps at peace.

Why would a ghost come to visit my kitchen? The history of Cahoon Farm offers an explanation. At one time, what is now the kitchen was divided, and inside of it was a small, sealed-off room. In that room, the family kept a patient—perhaps someone chronically ill, perhaps someone insane. It's uncertain. But in that tiny cell, the family member was cared for and kept safe.

It seems to me that the lady ghost must have had a deep devotion to the loved one in that room. She returns whenever something pulls her energy back, some change she needs to investigate, or the appearance of a visitor of whom she is unsure.

"Weren't you afraid?" I've been asked, upon telling the story. Of course I wasn't. Not at all. And neither was my friend's daughter. We all had someone watching over us with such tenderness and concern while we are alive to appreciate it.

Another Cahoon Farm Ghost Story

Madeline Hoffman Hall and her older sister grew up with the ghost of Daniel Cahoon, a distant ancestor. Apparently, he had a habit of stalking the halls of the historic homestead on East Lyndon Road.

The Georgian style home was finished around 1798 by Daniel Cahoon Jr, Daniel Cahoon's son, who was one of the town's settlers. Daniel Jr. died of tuberculosis at the young age of 26, and his father moved into the house.

A funeral alcove within the house. Madeline's family lived in the home years later. She was the the skeptic of the family and said that she never experienced any type of ghostly activity. Her bedroom was on the second floor and was the room where Daniel and other members of the family were "laid out" for funeral services after they passed away. Some in the family refer to the area as the "haunted chamber". Although Madeline claims that she herself never experienced anything unusual, others will not sleep there.

Two of her children claimed a haunting experience when the family occupied the house in the 1960's. They reported uneasy feelings within the second floor area and would not sleep there. Madeline's sister however, was an enthusiastic believer in ghosts and loved to share stories.

Most of the stories consisted of heavy footsteps up and down the stairs, while everyone was fast asleep. Kit Hoffman, Daniel's grandson 3 generations down, patiently tolerated the ghostly activities of his ancestor. His wife, however was a bit frightened when on a sub-zero morning, she awoke to the sound of a slamming front door, accompanied by door slams and heavy footsteps walking about the hallways. When confronted by his frightened wife, Kit said nonchalantly, "That's just Dan'l, our family ghost".

The playful poltergeist. Apparently, Daniel was quite the playful poltergeist. A ghost with a sense of humor! There was the story of a woman who stayed at the house one night, brushing her hair when suddenly the foot of the bed sunk as if an unseen person sat down. Another friend of the family, stayed the night and awoke in the middle of the night as something pulled the blankets away from her shoulders. This brought on a gentle tug of war between the guest and the ghost.

Another unusual event occurred when a friend was visiting and awoke to the sound of music playing. It seemed like 18th century music and eventually became louder. Nearby, she could hear gentle whispering voices, a woman's laughter and the distinct sound of glassware and silverware being moved about. Oddly enough the smell of snuff permeated the room. Perhaps ghostly memories being relived from days long past when dances and parties were held at the house?

As for Daniel himself, he was gored to death by a bull in 1811 at age 74, passing through the barnyard, (apparently while on a search for a wine cellar or more likely a still). His widow blamed his death on frequent visits to the "wine cellar" and had it boarded up. Nobody ever did find the actual location of the wine cellar after that.

From an article in Virginia Campbell Down's book, Mansions & Meadows, a book published in 1991 by the Lyndon Historical Society

Brattleboro, Vermont Hauntings

Brattleboro is Vermont's oldest town so it's not surprising that there may very well be a haunting or two in its long history.

At the Brattleboro, VT Austine School for the Deaf, security guards say that they have heard their names called when there was absolutely no one else present. Other staff members have been beckoned to in the same spot, all on different occasions. Other reports include a variety of strange noises. There is a strange uneasiness sometimes felt by those who work at the school.

Occasionally, "something" will pass by, momentarily visible just out of the corner of your eye. Lights turn on by themselves. A sense that you are being followed is not uncommon. When one turns around, nothing is there. Apparitions have been seen in mirrors and windows. Eerie shadows or vague ghostly faces sometimes become visible on the screens of televisions that are turned off. Fortunately no malevolent activity has ever been reported. Perhaps the ghostly residents are simply curious or concerned about the everyday activities at the school.

Another Brattleboro haunting? The country club in Brattleboro also has a haunted history. Wait staff and other workers report hearing footsteps or voices in the dining area but no one has yet to confirm the existence or possible origins of any spirits inhabiting the building.

Ricker Basin – A Vermont Ghost Town

Little River State Park is a Vermont State Park located on Little River Road, just off River Road between Bolton and Waterbury. Joseph Ricker established the community, back in the 1800's, on what was known as "Ricker Mountain". Rocks and stumps were cleared out and fields created in Ricker Basin and Cotton Brook. Later in the mid 1800's when the railroad made its way into Waterbury, the farming community began to take root in the area. Although the timber industry's 3 sawmills were the driving force for the small community, trading and other creative uses of local resources also helped people to get by. However, life was never easy at Ricker Basin (or Ricker Mills), for the 50 or so families that lived there. As the years passed into the late 1800's, families started to abandon their homes and land. The steep landscape and issues with soil quality made life on Ricker Mountain difficult.

The Waterbury Last Block Co., sawmill operated from 1916 until 1922 and was a resource for gunstocks and ammo cases for the First World War The mill at one time had 35 men working and a 44 teams of horses along with a truck. The steam powered sawmill came to an end in 1922 after its short run. A flood in 1927, caused by unceasing rainfall and rising waters, sealed the fate of the area forever. By 1934, another flood drove out the few families who had remained in the community after the first flood. This was also the time that prompted the construction of the Waterbury Dam and Reservoir that submerged much of what remained of the Ricker Basin community.

As of 2014, what remains of the community of Ricker Basin aka Ricker Mills is unfortunately, very little to nothing. The one house still standing is the Almeron Goodell Farm. It is a creepy, dilapidated and sad little house, open to the elements of nature and the carelessness of mankind. The roof is covered with moss and decay. The inside is covered with graffiti and ravaged by vandalism. The stench of age and bat guano fill the air with only peeks of sunlight peeking in through

roken windows. Restoration seems very unlikely and it will only be a
matter of time before this homestead is allowed to rot to its stone
foundations, like all of the other Ricker Basin farms in the abandoned
community.

Is Ricker Basin haunted?

There are those who claim that it is with some intriguing yarns that
supposedly back up that claim. One story is that a hunter went hiking
through the hills of Ricker Basin, camping out for a few nights, only to
experience some very unusual events. Fact or fiction? Who knows?
But like anything else, perhaps it wise not to "piss off fate", as the
poor fellow in the story goes on to explain how he inadvertently used
a broken headstone to construct a makeshift fire pit.

The Horrifying McCaffrey Murder at Cotton Brook

According to Mable Harvey, of Waterbury, VT., the Cotton Brook area
was also the scene of a grim murder. When the Civil War came to a
close, Matthew McCaffrey, a veteran of the war, returned home to
Greensboro, VT and took a wife. They moved to the Cotton Brook area
in Waterbury, where they all lived with his mother. The family
consisted of a son, daughter, twins and possibly other children.

They all resided in a farm house on a road with a brook running by
it, surrounded by an apple orchard. With acres of standing timber it
was an ideal place for McCaffrey to carry on work in lumber
operations.

However, all was not well. McCaffrey road horseback to
Waterbury one day with a chain around the neck of his horses,
claiming that the horses were going to kill his family. Naturally, the
neighbors thought was something was definitely amiss.

Madness leads to murder

Just a few nights later, McCaffrey thought he was hearing the cries of
wild animals. He took a light into the bedroom and told his older
children to look after the younger ones. He then proceeded to take an
ax and brutally kill both his wife and mother. Wrapping the bodies in

blankets, he carried them to the cellar. His 14 year old son either seeing or hearing the commotion, ran to the nearest neighbor for help. The bodies of the hapless victims were recovered by the authorities and buried in Greensboro.

Matthew McCaffrey was imprisoned but after the trail, he was moved for treatment to the Brattleboro Retreat. Eventually, he was moved to the Vermont State Hospital, where he remained confined for a total of 29 years. Cotton Brook is a remote area where only foundations of homes long gone, still remain. McCaffrey maintained an apple orchard and the trees are still there, on the right as you hike uphill.

Another sad murder in the area...
A child's gravestone located at the Duxbury Corner Cemetery reads: "Alice Meaker, April 18, 1880, aged nine years, eight months, nine days; Oh the agony and grief when the poisonous cup was given, and death came to her relief, and Alice sleeps in heaven."

Alice Meaker lived with her grandmother,at the top of Dillon Hill across from the present town clerk's office in Waterbury. Someone named "Uncle Almon" also resided in the Meaker home. Not much was known of the mysterious "Uncle Almon" who came to live with the family. It was much later believed that the grandmother fearing the child would communicate to easily with the "Uncle", decided to get rid of her.

What is known is that someone gave Alice poison. The person or persons then took her out of the house by night, carried her in a wagon to the Little River section and buried her body underground, partially under a trough and by a wet muddy swamp, known as Mutton Hollow.

Alice came up missing, so local farmers and residents started a search. They came upon her body with evidence indicating that she had not been dead when buried. Authorities arrested the grandmother along with "Uncle Almon". The grandmother was convicted of murder, becoming the first and only woman ever hung for murder in the state of Vermont.

Mr. Meaker wept openly during the trial. It is reported that in the courtroom there were some people who spat; "Damn you, you weep too late."

Uncle Almon was dispatched to State's Prison in Windsor, VT for a number of years. He was later pardoned and sent home to resume the remainder of his life.

Autumn hike at Ricker Basin

"Hiking Ricker Basin (or Ricker Mills) in late September 2014 was quite an experience. Certainly not a ghostly or ominous one. The air was crisp and clean on an unusually warm autumn day. There were only 2 or 3 other hikers around so it did feel a bit odd to be so alone there, as I was enjoying a solo hike. The long incline of the Hedgehog Hill Trail was a bit of a challenge due to the incline. The terrain itself was excellent but the long walk upwards wasn't nearly as easy as when I was 25 years old. I wish I would have had the time and energy to explore the entire area but a five mile hike was enough for me by day's end."

"At no time did I feel anything "haunted" or weird, even during a brief relaxation at the cemetery, where I pondered what life must have been like for these people back in those days. All of them now long dead for nearly 100 years. If anything, a feeling of comfort and peacefulness permeated the air with only the sounds of birds, the wind, swaying trees and crackling branches. It was lonely but in a good way that's hard to describe. I have to admit that I am very skeptical about the existence of ghosts. Where I to meet one, I'd probably have invited him or her to join me on my hike. I'd love to hear the stories of how these people lived and the hardships they endured."

"Yeah, a ghostly tour guide would have been perfect. I just don't think I would have wanted to meet one coming up from the basement of the Almeron Goodsell farm house! That place was truly creepy for safety reasons, especially when you're hiking solo."

Fall of Hyde Manor

A drive through the small town of Sudbury, VT, along Rte. 30, (one of those "don't blink or you'll miss it" Vermont towns) is pleasant enough and the bucolic scenery relaxing. I've made the drive many times myself on the way to work but one thing always seemed to pique my curiosity along the way...just for a second or two. As you're driving south on Rte 30, you'll see this magnificent, though decrepit building to your left, mostly hidden by trees. Yet, it still peeks out just enough to intrigue you and majestic enough to make you wonder just why such a building sits decaying in the middle of nowhere. For months, I wondered about this building and finally I stumbled across the answers.

The rapidly decaying building is officially known as Hyde Manor, a once grand antebellum resort hotel, now a crumbling shell of its former self. One can only wonder how majestic this structure was in its glory days. Constructed in 1865, its history originates as early as 1798. The Hyde Manor's origin was as a small place known as "Mills Tavern". In 1801, Pitt Hyde purchased the tavern and 47.5 surrounding acres. Hyde also owned a stage line that transported mail and passengers between Montréal and Albany. Back then Rte 30 was merely a roughhewn dirt road. In 1805, the stage road was upgraded into the Hubbardton Turnpike, (the equivalent of today's Route 7). The upgraded portion of the turnpike terminated at Hyde's Tavern, providing a huge business advantage. Pitt Hyde's son James, later took over the operation. He then commenced to offer all-night Yankee balls at the tavern which became very successful, creating a loyal customer following.

By the mid-century, James Hyde had established and improved the property, which then became known as Hyde's Hotel. New rail and water access made the area easily accessible to wealthy tourists in the mid 1800's. In addition to the scenic tranquility of the Vermont countryside, Hyde also promoted nearby mineral springs as "healing waters" which proved enticing to affluent travelers from the cities and urban areas. A fire decimated the building in 1862, providing the Hyde's with an opportunity to rebuild in a larger, more ornate fashion. This resulted in the regal Italianate building that still stands today. The resort became even more popular in the forthcoming years. The hotel was eventually passed down to James' son A.W. Hyde. A.W. again renovated and expanded the property, changing the name to Hyde Manor. Capacity was expanded to accommodate 300 guests (which at the time was more than half the population of Sudbury). New structures were added, such as the Casino, which offered a stage for live performances, and a circular building with a noticeably peaked roof. This odd little building was built specifically for a place for men to play cards. It has been restored and is still standing today. The Amusement Hall equipped with luxuries such as a bowling alley, billiard tables, a barber shop and dark room was also added. Hyde Manor also owned and hosted a 9 hole golf course across the road and a private boathouse on Lake Hortonia. Skiers could enjoy a ski hill and rope tow on a steep slope directly behind the hotel. After a long journey to the hills of Vermont, the Hyde Manor resort offered everything needed for a lengthy vacation getaway. Hyde Manor eventually became so popular that it usurped the town of Sudbury as the official location name.

All seemed well with the Hyde Manor resort, a majestic place where you could truly relax and enjoy a brief respite from everyday life. In the 1940's, the fall of the Hyde Manor began with a huge fire within the hotel's annex building, known as the largest in Sudbury's history. The resort continued to decline as improvements in travel, technology and progress offered people many more diverse travel options. The Hyde Manor's glory days were rapidly fading away as automobiles opened the way for small hotels, inns and other recreational options increased. The Hyde's eventually sold the resort

nd property in 1962. It operated as "The Top of the Seasons" until
970 when it eventually closed forever.

As of 2013, the formerly grand Hyde Resort is a fading memory of
:s glorious past, obscured by trees and overgrowth as the land takes
ack the property. The front of the hotel's "tower" is sagging and on
he verge of falling down. Sadly, most of the smaller buildings are
ecaying and being reclaimed by the surrounding foliage.

It's easy to drive by and think that the Hyde Manor is abandoned
nd vacant but oddly enough it's not. One of the small buildings is
ccupied by its current owners who could not afford to renovate or
ven demolish the resort. As tempting as it might be to explore, be
ware that the property is occupied and it's doubtful that the owners
ould welcome intruders, ghost busters or curiosity seekers. I would
ke to thank Chad Abramovich at *Urban Post Mortem* for his gracious
ermission and invaluable help in preparing this article. Chad has a
ealth of info and photos about the Hyde Manor, which is simply
antastic.

Abandoned Air Force Base

The abandoned North Concord Radar Station, Air Force base located high in the hills of East Haven, VT has always been an intriguing location. The base became operational in 1956 and was renamed the Lyndonville AFS in 1962. The site and its operations were closed by the Air Force in 1963, leaving many of the buildings standing but decaying into disrepair over the years. The town of East Haven grew in size around the area. In 1961, the station reported a UFO sighting that lasted 18 minutes and occurred just a few hours before the alleged UFO abduction of Barney and Betty Hill, in nearby New Hampshire. The former base is located on a 17 acre parcel of land which could have literally been the top of a mountain peak, leveled to create the Station and its surrounding buildings. The base camp was located a few miles below on a 30 acres parcel.

Deaths at the Radar Base

In 1969, four years after the base was purchased by the late Ed Sawyer of East Burke, snowmobilers were using the property without permission when one of the snowmobilers hit a chain slung across the road and was decapitated. About 23 years ago, someone roaming the property died in a fall from one of the buildings. There have also been a number of shootings there. It's as though the Cold War mentality that surrounded the base's hurried construction continues to bring out the worst in people. "Something changes when you get up here" said Ed Sawyer, who was a former owner of the property that he purchased from the federal government in 1965 for $41,500.

www.ingramcontent.com/pod-product-compliance
Lightning Source LLC
Chambersburg PA
CBHW031423250726
48656CB00002B/799